TABLE OF CONTENTS

W9-BHB-164

Slim Goodbody's
LIGHTEN UP
SERIES

HELLO THERE. I'M SLIM GOODBODY,

and my greatest goal in life is to help young people across the planet become healthy and active. After all, one in three kids in the United States is overweight. Without changing their eating and exercise habits, many of these young people will become overweight adults. They risk many possible health problems like **high blood pressure** or **diabetes.**

Today, I would like to introduce you to my friend Martina. Martina is a high school student. This summer, she worked as an **intern** at an **advertising agency**. She is going give us an inside look at the world of advertising. We will learn about the ways advertisements influence our decisions to buy things. She will also share what she learned about making good choices and setting goals for a healthier lifestyle.

ADS, ADS, EVERYWHERE

Hi! My name is Martina. Ever since I was a little kid, I've liked watching commercials on TV and looking at glossy advertisements in magazines. The bright colors, fun music, and famous people in the ads always grabbed my attention. I wanted to buy what was being shown. This summer, I decided to apply to be an intern at my uncle's advertising agency. I wanted to see how advertising developed.

Why Buy?

When a company makes something, whether it's basketball shoes or candy bars, they need to find a way to get people to choose their product. The company uses ads to show how their product is special and why everyone should buy it. Found everywhere — from on TV to the side of a bus — the ads are designed to be **persuasive**. Have you ever bought something at the store because you liked the ad for it on TV? Most of us have.

So you see, advertising works!

ADVERTISING TRICKS

Crabtree Publishing Company
www.crabtreebooks.com

Series Development and Packaging: John Burstein, Slim Goodbody Corp.
Senior Script Development: Phoebe Backler
Managing Editor: Valerie J. Weber
Designer and Illustrator: Ben McGinnis
Graphic Design Agency: Adventure Advertising
Instructional Designer: Alan Backler, Ph. D.
Content Consultant: Betty Hubbard, Ed. D., Certified Health Education Specialist
Project Editor: Reagan Miller

Library and Archives Canada Cataloguing in Publication

Burstein, John.
    Big fat lies : advertising tricks / Slim Goodbody.

(Slim Goodbody's lighten up!)
ISBN 978-0-7787-3913-5 (bound).--ISBN 978-0-7787-3931-9 (pbk.)

    1. Advertising--Food--Juvenile literature. I. Title. II. Series:
Goodbody,
Slim. Slim Goodbody's lighten up!
HF6161.F616G66 2008   j659.19'6413
C2008-900725-5

Library of Congress Cataloging-in-Publication Data

Burstein, John.
    Big fat lies : advertising tricks / John Burstein.
        p. cm. -- (Slim Goodbody's lighten up!)
    Includes index.
    ISBN-13: 978-0-7787-3913-5 (rlb)
    ISBN-10: 0-7787-3913-9 (rlb)
    ISBN-13: 978-0-7787-3931-9 (pb)
    ISBN-10: 0-7787-3931-7 (pb)
    1. Advertising--Food--Juvenile literature. I. Title. II. Series.
HF6161.F616B87 2008
659.1'11--dc22
                                    2008003592

Crabtree Publishing Company

www.crabtreebooks.com   1-800-387-7650

Published in Canada
Crabtree Publishing
616 Welland Ave.
St. Catharines, Ontario
L2M 5V6

Published in the United States
Crabtree Publishing
PMB16A
350 Fifth Ave., Suite 3308
New York, NY 10118

Published in the United Kingdom
Crabtree Publishing
White Cross Mills
High Town, Lancaster
LA1 4XS

Published in Australia
Crabtree Publishing
386 Mt. Alexander Rd.
Ascot Vale (Melbourne)
VIC 3032

"Slim Goodbody" and "Lighten Up with Slim Goodbody" are registered trademarks of the Slim Goodbody Corp.

Printed in the U.S.A.

While working at the advertising agency, I learned that American kids watch an average of 40,000 TV commercials each year! And TV is just one place where people see advertisements. Most kids in the United States spend about eight hours every day listening, reading, or watching media, including radio, TV, Internet, books, magazines, newspapers, video games, movies, and music! Imagine how many advertisements they come across during those eight hours!

NO DOWNSIDE IN ADS

The most important lesson I learned this summer is that you can't rely on advertisements to make healthy choices about what to buy. Why? Ads never tell the whole story or include information about the negative side of a product. You don't see ads for fast-food restaurants talking about the health problems people often get if they eat too many burgers and French fries, right? You have to find other ways to learn about products before you buy them.

Now, let's explore the world of advertising and healthy decision-making!

Slim's
STAGGERING
STATISTICS

By the age of 65, most Americans have seen two million TV commercials!

WILL YOU HOP ON THE BANDWAGON?

During my first week at the ad agency, I learned that I would be working with a team to create a new **advertising campaign** for Coco Chunk Cereal. Our job was to come up with ideas for how to make Coco Chunk Cereal seem new and exciting. We wanted kids to see our ads and immediately want to eat a bowl of our cereal.

"OK!" said Carl, the team leader, "Let's get started! Does anybody have ideas about how to make it seem cool to eat Coco Chunk Cereal?"

THE CAMPAIGN TO SEEM COOL

One team member suggested, "What about a TV commercial with students talking at school about how Coco Chunk Cereal is the most delicious cereal they've ever eaten? If the students in the commercial are good-looking, well dressed, and look like they're having a great time together, it will seem like eating Coco Chunk Cereal is cool. If kids at home believe that the cereal helps them be cool, they'll want to buy it."

"Yeah, I like that!" said another team member. "We could also put Coco Chunk Cereal stickers inside every box. In the commercial, the cool kids can have Coco Chunk Cereal stickers on their backpacks. It will make them seem like they're part of a cool club. That way, the kids at home will want to get on the **bandwagon** and become part of the club too."

Another team member suggested, "What if the commercial included a kid who didn't fit in watching the rest of the group talk about their breakfasts? The next morning, he comes to school with a Coco Chunk Cereal sticker on his backpack. Suddenly, the kid is hanging out with the group. The image will imply that being seen with a Coco Chunk sticker will make you cool. You'll be accepted by anyone, even the popular kids."

"Great," said Carl. "I think we're on to something here. We want kids to get the message that Coco Chunk Cereal is not only delicious, but it will make them more popular, too."

DOES THE CAMPAIGN REALLY WORK?

"But that's not true, is it?" I asked. "Just because you eat a certain kind of cereal doesn't mean that you will have more friends."

"Do you like the same kinds of food as your friends?" asked Carl.

"I guess so," I replied, "but that isn't why we're friends."

Carl sighed, "That doesn't matter. If kids believe us, and they buy our cereal, we have done our job. That's what advertising is all about, Martina. We can't lie, but we need to persuade people that they should buy our product. The best way to do that is to tell them that Coco Chunk Cereal will help them have the life they want."

WANT TO SING A JINGLE?

I didn't like telling kids that Coco Chunk Cereal was their ticket to having more friends and to being popular. I didn't have a chance to worry about this; Carl was calling for our attention again.

Coco Chunk Campaign Ideas:
✓ Stickers In Box
✓ A Jingle or Slogan

"OK," said Carl, "Now we need to work on a **jingle** or song for Coco Chunk Cereal. It should be funny and simple, but most importantly, it has to be catchy. We want kids to hear the Coco Chunk Cereal jingle once and then sing it at school or in the car. We especially want them to think of it at the grocery store when they go shopping with their parents! Every time they sing the jingle, kids will think about our cereal and want to eat some."

A RAP TO REMEMBER

The rest of the team thought hard. One of the team members suggested, "We should stick with the idea that eating Coco Chunk Cereal is the cool thing to do. What about having the students in the commercial start doing a free-style rap? They could say something like . . .

'It's cool and funky,
It's coco chunky,
Tell your mom,
This cereal's the bomb!
I've gotta get some Coco Chunks!'"

"That's great! Can we add any sound effects?" asked Carl. "The more exciting and fun it is, the more it will grab kids' attention."

"Let's have the box of Coco Chunk Cereal explode. Cereal can rain all over the students when they say 'this cereal's the bomb,'" suggested one of the team members.

"Perfect! Good work, everyone. This campaign is really coming together," said Carl.

WHO DO YOU TRUST?

The next day, Carl called us back together. "Something's still missing," he said. "We need another way to grab kids' attention and convince them to try Coco Chunk Cereal. Any ideas?"

A team member spoke up. "What if we got a spokesperson? We could hire someone famous to **endorse** Coco Chunk Cereal. We could even have his or her picture on the box. Who should we use?"

STAYING ON TARGET

"It has to be someone that would appeal to kids," offered another team member. "But it depends on our **target audience** or what kinds of kids we are appealing to. Jennifer Lopez would really appeal to Latino kids. Of course, she is so famous now that most kids like her. If kids think that she eats our cereal, they'll buy it so they can be more like her. Of course, boys would be more drawn to a sports star. What about Derek Jeter, the short stop for the New York Yankees?"

I interrupted. "I'm kind of offended by this conversation. Just because I'm Latina doesn't mean that I like Jennifer Lopez. In fact, I would trust a professional athlete's opinion about nutrition more than hers!"

Carl started to explain, "Martina, this kind of thing goes on all the time in advertising. We have to look at our **market**. We look at the age and sometimes the race of the people who will buy our product. In this case, our market is kids, right? We have to find a spokesperson who will attract as many kids as possible. We then pay the spokesperson to say that he or she likes our product."

Coco Chunk
Campaign Ideas:

✓ Stickers In Box

✓ A Jingle or Slogan

✓ Using Product
  Makes Kid Cool

✓ Rap Jingle

✓ Spokesperson? Who?

COCO CHUNKS CEREAL

Nutritious & Delicious!

APPEALING TO THE AUDIENCE

Another team member suggested, "I think that we should use a cartoon character instead. We should create something that is cute and cuddly to appeal to girls. It can also be mischievous and get into a lot of trouble to appeal to boys."

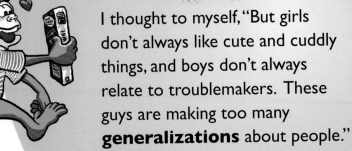

I thought to myself, "But girls don't always like cute and cuddly things, and boys don't always relate to troublemakers. These guys are making too many **generalizations** about people."

"I know!" shouted another teammate. "What if we create a chocolate-loving monkey? He does tricks so the kids reward him with Coco Chunk Cereal. He can get into trouble because he is always trying to do wild and crazy things to get more cereal. Of course, he will be cute and loveable, too. The Coco Chunk monkey would appeal to both boys and girls."

COCO CHUNKS CEREAL

"The Coco Chunk monkey it is!" said Carl. "Good work, team."

LIKE THE LOOK?

"Our next job is to come up with ways of describing Coco Chunk Cereal. Remember, we are actually appealing to kids and their parents. Kids should want to eat our cereal, but moms and dads are the people who are buying it. Let's start with ideas to attract the kids," said Carl.

DESCRIBE
COCO CHUNKS CEREAL

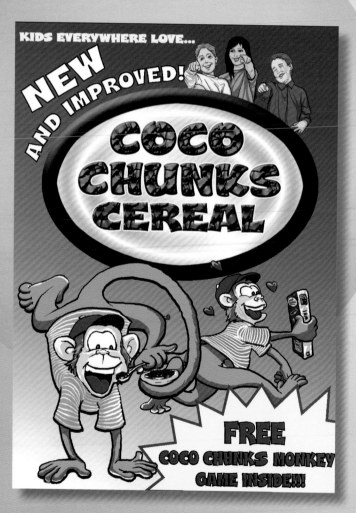

KIDS EVERYWHERE LOVE...
NEW AND IMPROVED!
COCO CHUNKS CEREAL
FREE COCO CHUNKS MONKEY GAME INSIDE!!!

CHARMING THE CHILDREN

The rest of the team **brainstormed**, and one person offered, "What if we make the cereal box out of something shiny? It could have games and comics on the back, too. If the box looks fun, exciting, and different, it will grab kids' attention. Then they'll be more likely to ask their parents to buy our cereal."

Another team member suggested, "We can also use words like 'new and improved' on the box. Kids always want to try the newest products on the shelves. Maybe we can include something like 'Kids everywhere love Coco Chunk Cereal!' If kids think everyone around them loves Coco Chunk Cereal, they will too."

"I think we should offer a toy inside the box. What about a simple Coco Chunk Monkey video game? It doesn't cost much money to make a simple video game, but it will give kids another reason to want our cereal," said another teammate.

Slim Goodbody Says: You've probably seen messages like "Great Value! Now 50% more!" written on potato chip bags or cookie boxes. It seems like a great deal because you are getting more for your money. The truth is that it doesn't cost the company very much to add the extra food. It's just another way to get you to buy the product. The same goes for those super-sized portions of popcorn at the movie theater or super-sized French fries at the restaurant. The huge portions might seem appealing, but they are very unhealthy. The excess **calories** and fats are not good for your body.

WHAT PARENTS WANT

"Great," said Carl. "Now, what are parents looking for?"

One of the team members chimed in, "Parents want their kids to be healthy. The cereal box should have descriptions such as 'all natural,' 'low fat,' and 'whole grain' on it. Parents also hate to fight with their kids about eating **nutritious** foods. We should say something like, 'A healthy choice that your kids will love.'"

I was confused. "But is Coco Chunk cereal actually healthy?" I asked.

"Well, Martina, it depends on what you consider healthy," laughed Carl. "I wouldn't feed Coco Chunk cereal to my kids; it has loads of sugar in it. It also has some vitamins and minerals, so we can get away with saying that it is nutritious. Remember, we are trying to sell this cereal and make money. We can't advertise that Coco Chunk Cereal is all sugar and no nutrients."

"I guess not," I said, but it seemed wrong to make parents think our cereal was healthy.

DOES THIS FOOD HAVE STYLE?

The next day, I learned that a **food stylist** was coming in to talk with us about how to make Coco Chunk Cereal look great in photographs on the box. A food stylist tries to make the food in pictures look so delicious that people will want to run out and buy it.

"Okay, gang." said Carl. "This is Julie, our food stylist."

WANT SOME GLUE FOR YOUR CEREAL?

"Let's get started," said Julie. "Cereal is difficult to prepare for photographs because it turns to mush in milk. It can take hours to get the right picture in a photo shoot. You have to use some tricks to keep the cereal looking fresh and delicious. Some food stylists use glue instead of milk because it doesn't soak into the cereal flakes. I also suggest opening up seven or eight boxes of Coco Chunk cereal and sorting through them. You have to find the best, most perfectly shaped Coco Chunks to make the photos look great."

White glue instead of milk! No wonder my bowl of cereal never looks as good as the one on the box. "Julie, can you share some of your tricks for preparing other kinds of food for photo shoots?" I asked.

Photo Shoot Tricks

Julie smiled, "Well, ice cream is difficult to photograph because it melts quickly. I use mashed potatoes or lard with food coloring instead of ice cream. It can be hard to make meat look picture perfect. I always bring along my blowtorch to give it a nice charred look. I've even rearranged the sesame seeds on a hamburger bun to look as delicious as possible. It might seem strange, but we take these steps to convince people to buy our products."

"Wow!" I laughed. "The next time I see an ad for food, I'm going to find out if I can tell what the food stylist did to make it look so appealing."

ADVERTISING STRATEGIES

Once school started, I wanted to visit my health teacher from last year, Mrs. Simon. I was excited to talk to her about what I had learned. I especially wanted to tell her about the different ways advertisers try to convince people to buy their products:

• The bandwagon approach attempts to convince people that they should buy a product if they want to be cool and fit in.

• A jingle or catchy phrase helps keep people thinking about the product. This device increases the chance that they will buy the product when they go to the store.

It's cool and funky.
It's coco chunky.
Tell your mom,
This cereal's the bomb!
I've gotta get some Coco Chunks!

• Paying someone famous to be a spokesperson and to say great things about a product is another way to convince people to buy something.

• Instead of hiring a famous person, some advertisers create a cartoon character to be the spokesperson for a product. Ads with cartoon characters often appeal to kids because they can relate to the cuddly, fun animals.

• The language that advertisers use is carefully chosen to appeal to their market.

• Food stylists make the product look perfect for photographs. If the picture of a bowl of cereal on the box looks fresh, delicious, and larger than life, people will want to buy that brand of cereal.

"I guess I have a lot to talk about with Mrs. Simon!" I thought.

Slim Goodbody Says: The next time you watch TV, look for these advertising techniques. List the different ways the advertisement makes the product look **irresistible**. Is the ad working? Do you want to buy the product it is selling? Tell your parents and siblings what you are doing and have them make their own lists of the advertising strategies they see on TV.

ANALYZING ADS

At school, I shared what I'd learned about advertising with my health teacher, Mrs. Simon.

"My goodness, Martina! What an education you got this summer! Most people never learn about advertising strategies. Supermodels tell people that they will be happier if they buy a certain kind of skin cream, and they believe it! Now that you know what tools advertisers use, you can learn how to read an advertisement," said Mrs. Simon.

"What do you mean?" I asked.

"When you read an advertisement, you look for the ways that advertisers are trying to influence you. The first step is to ask yourself what strategy are the advertisers using to make their product seem desirable. The second step is to figure out what the strategy is intended to do. The last step is to ask how will this strategy influence behavior," explained Mrs. Simon.

POOCH SELLS POTATO CHIP

She turned on the television over her desk. An advertisement came on. A cartoon dog was bouncing around and talking about Ralph's delicious, all-natural potato chips.

Mrs. Simon turned to me. "What do you see in this advertisement? What strategy are the advertisers using to make their product seem desirable?"

"Well, they used a cartoon dog to make the potato chips seem fun and harmless."

"And who is the cartoon likely to appeal to?" asked Mrs. Simon.

"Kids will be attracted to the cartoon character," I answered.

"Right, and how will the cartoon influence behavior?" she asked.

"If the kids like the ad and the cartoon, they will ask their parents to buy the chips," I explained.

"Very good! What else did you notice?" asked Mrs. Simon.

NOT A HEALTHY SNACK

"The advertisers also described the chips as all natural and low fat. That strategy is intended to convince parents that the potato chips are nutritious. It is trying to influence the parents' behavior by making them feel good about buying the chips. Of course, that doesn't mean that the chips are nutritious. If they are cooked in oil and covered in salt, then they are not a healthy snack for anyone!"

"Exactly," said Mrs. Simon.

Slim Goodbody Says: The next time you watch TV, use Mrs. Simon's three steps to read the advertisements you see. Ask yourself:
• What is the strategy?
• What is it intended to do?
• How will it influence behavior?
• Once you have read the advertisement, decide for yourself if you think the product is worth buying.

FINDING OUT ABOUT HEALTHY FOODS

"So now you know how to view ads critically and look for misleading messages. You're ready to learn the next step," said Mrs. Simon

"What's that?" I asked.

"Learning how to be a **health consumer** and choose foods that are good for you," said Mrs. Simon. "But you'll have to do some research. There are all sorts of **valid**, reliable resources to help you learn about what products to buy. At the library, you can find books, magazines, and pamphlets about nutrition and health written by the American Heart Association, the American Cancer Society, and other health groups. You can also find information on products written by **consumer groups**," said Mrs. Simon.

"What's a consumer group?" I asked.

"A consumer group researches and tests products. These people rate all sorts of different things, from hand lotion to cars, based on their value and quality," she explained.

"The Internet probably has a lot of useful information about products too," I added.

A MATTER OF TRUST

"Absolutely. But you have to know where to look. Not every Web site has accurate information. When you are doing research on the Internet, it is safest to look for Web sites that end with .gov or .edu. Those initials mean that they are funded by the government or an educational institution," said Mrs. Simon.

"I see. The government and schools aren't trying to sell you products, so you can trust their information," I said.

.GOV
.EDU

"Right. Companies sometimes send out information about their product that is often inaccurate or incomplete," agreed Mrs. Simon.

"I can always come and ask you for your advice about a product too, right?" I asked.

"Of course! Teachers, school nurses, your doctor, and adults in your family can all help you be a health consumer."

"Thanks, Mrs. Simon."

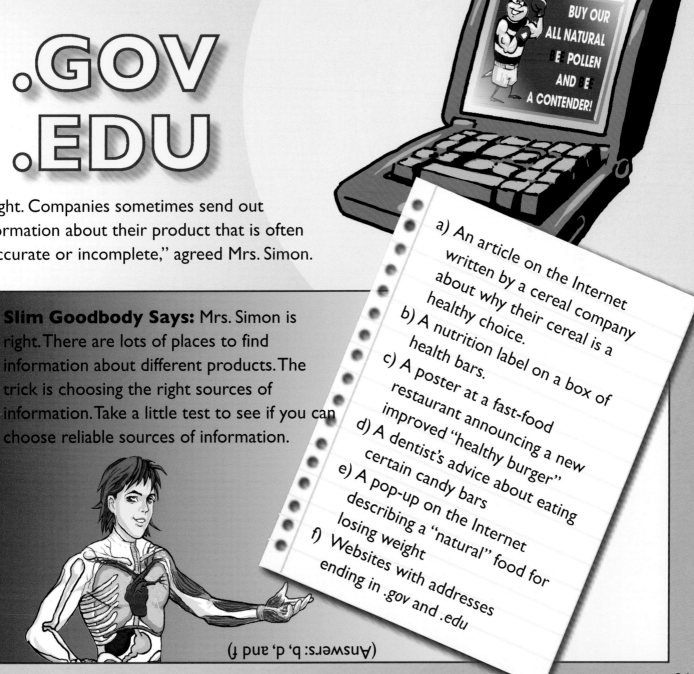

Slim Goodbody Says: Mrs. Simon is right. There are lots of places to find information about different products. The trick is choosing the right sources of information. Take a little test to see if you can choose reliable sources of information.

a) An article on the Internet written by a cereal company about why their cereal is a healthy choice.

b) A nutrition label on a box of health bars.

c) A poster at a fast-food restaurant announcing a new improved "healthy burger"

d) A dentist's advice about eating certain candy bars

e) A pop-up on the Internet describing a "natural" food for losing weight

f) Websites with addresses ending in .gov and .edu

(Answers: b, d, and f)

21

MAKING A GREAT DECISION

After school that day, I wondered, "How can I make sure that I use these skills every time I buy something? I know, the next time I go to the store, I can use a simple decision-making process to choose the best product available."

FIRST, I will *identify my choices*. I will look at the different products I can choose from.

SECOND, I'll *evaluate each choice*. I'll use the valid information that I have collected about healthy, high-quality products from my doctor, the library, my parents, and the Internet. I will also look for healthy ingredients on the nutrition label on the food package.

THIRD, I will *identify the healthiest decision* by using the information I have gathered and comparing the different products.

FOURTH, I will be ready to *take action* and buy the healthiest and highest-quality product available.

FINALLY, after using the product, I will *evaluate my decision*. I'll decide if I should buy the same product again.

22

A Real-Life Test

All this thinking was making me hungry, so I went to the store to test my decision-making process. First, I identified my choices and saw that I could buy some cookies, a box of whole-wheat crackers, or a bag of potato chips.

Next I evaluated each choice by looking at the nutrition label on each package. Remembering my health teacher and doctor's advice, I looked at the **fat content** and the number of calories. I also checked to see if there were unhealthy ingredients like **hydrogenated oils** and **high-fructose corn syrup** in each of the snacks.

Then, I identified the healthiest choice. I saw that the whole-wheat crackers had the best ingredients and the fewest calories.

Next, I took action by buying just the crackers. Finally, I evaluated my decision. After eating my crackers, I noticed that I felt great and had more energy than before.

"They tasted really good, too. I think I'll buy the crackers again next time," I said to myself.

Slim Goodbody Says: The next time you are at the store, try using these simple steps to make a smart decision about what to buy! Make sure you check out how you feel afterward and what you would do in the future.

SETTING AND GETTING TO YOUR GOALS

When I got home, I told my mother all about my conversation with Mrs. Simon and my new decision-making process.

"I am so proud of you, Martina. Learning how to make healthy choices is an important part of growing up and becoming a healthy adult."

"But it feels like a lot of work to make smart decisions every time I choose something to eat, Mom. What if I make a mistake or can't convince myself that the healthy choice is the right choice?"

"Martina, you have to be realistic. No one is perfect. We all make mistakes and buy things that are bad for us from time to time. Just set goals for yourself and try your hardest to reach your them. Let's write down your goals together."

THE BIG PLAN

"First, think of a realistic goal and write it down," said Mom. "If your goal is 'I will make healthy choices all the time,' you are setting yourself up to fail. It's helpful to make your goal measurable too. For instance, you can decide to work toward your goal for a certain amount of time."

"My goal is to try to eat healthy cereal for the next two weeks," I decided.

"That's a great idea," responded my mother. "What steps must you take to achieve that goal?"

"First, I won't pick a cereal because of the packaging or because of its cool ad on TV. I will use my new decision-making process to choose a healthy cereal." I wrote down the steps I needed to take to achieve my goal.

"Great," said my mother. "The next step is to get help and support from others."

"Well, I can tell my friends about my goal. It would be fun to work on the same goal together. We can help each other!" I said. "Will you buy healthy cereal for me too? Then I won't be tempted to eat sugary cereal."

"Of course! And after two weeks, you can evaluate your progress. If you met your goal of eating healthy cereal the whole time, you can reward yourself. Try to make healthy choices about your rewards as well as your goals. You could go to the movies with your friends or have a sleepover." said my mother.

Slim Goodbody Says: Setting goals is a great way to work towards a healthy lifestyle. Are you ready to give it a try? It's easy! Just follow Martina's five basic steps:
- Set a realistic, measurable goal and write it down
- List the steps to reach the goal
- Get help/support from others
- Evaluate your progress
- Reward yourself

BECOMING A HEALTH ADVOCATE

The next week, my mother, my brother Ronnie and I were watching TV. The ad for Coco Chunk Cereal popped up on the screen. The Coco Chunk Monkey jumped in circles, and the kids with the stickers on their backpacks laughed. At the end of the ad, a close-up picture of the cereal made it look absolutely delicious. The food stylist had done a great job.

DON'T BELIEVE EVERYTHING YOU SEE

"That looks so good. Let's go buy a box. I'm hungry," said Ronnie, getting off the couch.

"Sit down, Ronnie. That cereal is not good for you. It has too much sugar in it," I laughed.

"Come on. That song is so great! Plus the ad said that it's healthy. It can't have that much sugar in it!"

"Oh, Ronnie," I sighed. "You have to learn not to believe everything you see and hear in advertisements."

TAKING A STAND

My mother turned to me. "Martina, I think you are ready to become a health advocate, someone who encourages others to develop a healthy lifestyle and make good choices."

"I'm ready, Mom. How do I start?"

"Well the first step is to *take a healthy stand on an issue*. Helping others to become health consumers seems to be your passion. Then *persuade others to make a healthy choice*. Use what you now know about advertising, decision-making, and goal setting to help others learn how to be health consumers. Finally, you have to *be convincing!* You are passionate and know a lot about this issue. It should be easy to get others to see why they should be health consumers like you."

Slim Goodbody Says: Can you imagine yourself as a health advocate? You can be very effective if you use these easy steps:

• Take a healthy stand on an issue
• Persuade others to make a healthy choices using valid information from school, your parents or your doctor
• Be convincing

A HEALTHY MESSAGE

Mom, I know how to be convincing! I learned all sorts of tricks to influence people at the advertising agency this summer. I can use those techniques to spread a healthy message! I can even write my own jingle about how to make healthy choices. What about:

Hey there, kid,
Don t be a fool,
Coco Chunk Cereal
Won t make you cool!

You ve got to be smart
And use your brain
Or else those ads
Will make you insane!

Look on the label
Or ask your doc
Making healthy choices
Is how to rock!

 **Slim Goodbody Says:** How will you spread your healthy message? You can make bumper stickers or posters or offer daily health announcements over the loudspeaker at school. Remember, if you know about the issue and you are creative and passionate, people will listen!

TOWARD A HEALTHIER LIFESTYLE

I went up to my room to think more about becoming a health advocate. I could use advertising methods to spread a healthy message.

Mrs. Simon had asked me to make a mind map of what I had learned this summer. I realized that everything I had learned — about making healthy choices, being a health consumer, reading advertisements, setting healthy goals and being a health advocate — was all related.

"If I use the lessons I've learned this summer, I can work toward a healthier lifestyle," I thought to myself.

"That's it! Working towards a healthier lifestyle will be the central idea for my mind map."

FIND VALID SOURCES OF INFORMATION ABOUT NUTRITION AND PRODUCTS THROUGH

the library
your parents
your health teacher
your doctor
Web sites with addresses
ending in .gov or .edu

DIFFERENT STRATEGIES OF ADVERTISERS

Bandwagon approach
Jingle or slogan
Spokesperson
Language like "New and Improved! and "Low Fat"
Food styling

Work toward a healthier lifestyle

BECOME A HEALTH ADVOCATE

Take a healthy stand on an issue
Persuade others to make healthy choices
Be convincing

LEARN HOW TO READ ADVERTISEMENTS

What is the strategy?
What is the strategy intended to do?
How will it influence behavior?

SPREAD YOUR MESSAGE

Perform a skit about making healthy
choices for your class
Make posters about your issue and
put them up around school
Make bumper stickers with a healthy message

Slim Goodbody Says: Now it's your turn to review what you have learned here. Make a poster or a create a skit, including everything you've learned about advertising, making healthy decisions, and being a health advocate from Martina. If YOU use the lessons from this book, you'll be working toward a healthier lifestyle too!

Glossary

advertising agency A business that creates advertisements about different products

advertising campaign A series of advertisements made for everything from magazines to billboards to promote a product

bandwagon Refers to an advertising method that tries to convince people that they should use a product because it is fashionable and everyone else uses it

brainstorm To discuss various possible solutions to a problem with a group of people

calorie Unit of food energy; calories that are not burned through metabolic processes or physical activity are stored in the body as fat

consumer groups Groups that research, test, and rate the quality of products

diabetes A disease in which a person has too much sugar in their blood. A person with diabetes cannot produce enough insulin, the substance the body needs to use sugar properly.

endorse To give approval or support to something

fat content A measurement on the food label telling how much and what kind of fats a product contains

food stylist Someone who arranges food to be attractively photographed

generalization A sweeping statement that assigns specific characteristics to a large group whether those characteristics are valid or not for individuals in that group

health consumer Someone who knows about nutrition and chooses healthy kinds of food

health blood pressure A condition that forces the heart to work too hard to pump blood.

high-fructose corn syrup A specially treated sweetener made from corn that appears in many foods

hydrogenated oils Oils, such as butter, that stay in solid form at room temperature

intern A student who works in a usually unpaid position in an organization to gain practical experience

irresistible Impossible to fight against or withstand

jingle A short, catchy song that reminds people of a product when they hear it

market A specific category of people who might buy a product

nutritious Providing nutrients, things that people, other animals, and plants need to live

persuasive Able to convince someone about an issue

target audience A specific group of people that advertisers are trying to attract

valid Based in facts

FOR FURTHER INFORMATION

Media Awareness Network: Common Advertising Strategies

www.media-awareness.ca/english/resources/educational/handouts/advertising_marketing/common_ad_strats.cfm

Learn ten different strategies that advertisers use to convince people to buy their product.

PBS Kids Go: Don't Buy It — Get Media Smart — Advertising Tricks

pbskids.org/dontbuyit/advertisingtricks/foodadtricks.html

Learn more about the tricks food stylists use to make food look tempting in advertisements.

PBS Kids Go: Don't Buy It — Get Media Smart — Buying Smart

pbskids.org/dontbuyit/buyingsmart

Discover more about reading advertisements and becoming a smart shopper.

Centers for Disease Control and Prevention: Ad Decoder

www.bam.gov/sub_yourlife/yourlife_addecoder.html

Learn more about reading advertisements. You can be an ad detective and crack the coded messages being sent by advertisers.

INDEX

ABOUT THE AUTHOR

John Burstein (also known as Slim Goodbody) has been entertaining and educating children for over thirty years. His programs have been broadcast on CBS, PBS, Nickelodeon, USA, and Discovery. He has won numerous awards including the Parent's Choice Award and the President's Council's Fitness Leader Award. Currently, Mr. Burstein tours the country with his live multimedia show "Bodyology." For more information, please visit slimgoodbody.com